Places Near and Far

by

Robert Harlow

Louisiana Literature Press
Hammond, Louisiana

Printed in the United States of America
FIRST EDITION, 2018

Cover Art: "Four Bowls near Where Water Falls." Ceramic art by Nancy K. Henry. Photo credit: Nancy K. Henry

Author's Photo: Nancy K. Henry

Requests for Permission to reproduce material from this work should be sent to: Louisiana Literature Press
SLU Box 10792
Hammond, LA 70402

Acknowledgments

Grateful acknowledgment is made to the editors of the journals in which these poems, often in earlier versions, first appeared:

The Albany Review: "Patience"
Connecticut River Review: "First Snow"
Cottonwood: "Out Here," Heritage"
Foxtail: "In Japan"
The Midwest Quarterly: "Close to Home," The Comet," "Guided Tour," "Heartland," "Home," "Similes for the Sun"
Mildred: "A Momentary Stay," "Pantoum Beginning with a Line by Louise Bogan"
Poetry Northwest: "Doors," "Mr. Moto Takes a Vacation"

Notes:

The first line of "Pantoum Beginning with a Line from Louise Bogan" is the first line of her poem "Women."

The haiku at the beginning of "Snow" was written by Arō in mid 18th century Japan.

"Mr. Moto Takes a Vacation" is the title of a 1939 film starring Peter Lorre. I have not seen the film, so if the poem resembles the film, it is a miraculous coincidence.

"The Tooker Paintings," in Section II, are based on the paintings done by George Tooker (1920-2011), American figurative painter in the so-called Magic Realism style.

Each stanza of "Songs for the Tropics" begins with a slight variation of a line in "Anecdote of Men By the Thousand" by Wallace Stevens.

"Parting" contains the poem written in 14th century Japan by Lady Sono No Omi Ikuha. It can be found in Kenneth Rexroth's *One Hundred More Poems from the Japanese.*

"W/Reckless Love" contains the title of the painting *I Love You with My Ford* (1961) by James Rosenquist. The poem does not reflect the content of the painting or vice versa.

Thanks:

First to Don Johnson who has been there with encouragement from the beginning and who has remained a good friend and reader for more than forty years. Next is to Jordan Smith who has offered unwavering support ever since we've known each other. And to Donald Revell for shining a light along the way. Three fine poets who teach me still.

But most importantly is my debt and endless love to my wife, the ceramic artist, Nancy K. Henry, her delicate hands helping me on the journey from there to here in this marriage of poet and potter, no difference between us, between our hands in our travels to and from places near and far.

This book, these poems, are for her.

for

Nancy K. Henry

CONTENTS

IV. Close to Home

I.
Home

W/Reckless Love

So it all comes down to this:
I love you with my Ford.
Think of my devotion
as an experiment of choices,
something to prove I'm not afraid
of commitment, at least for tonight.
And think of this little tremor
of my hand on the wheel
as a place to begin.

I mean, I can drive this thing
all day with just one hand,
the other resting on the side-view mirror.
Perhaps I'll turn the radio on.
With some luck maybe Sinatra
will be there to tell us
how sad the night can be
when you're alone
and how it changes when the danger
of love gets real close.

This is how it is:
I'm tall and slender,
and although I sometimes wear a beard,
this car has real smooth fenders
that shine as these tires whistle
through the streetlights.

So what do you say
to this romance, this torrent
of steel? Let's go
where rust can't find us,
where chamois is our friend,
even if we have to run
some stoplights along the way.

Suppose I just take my hands
off the wheel and put them
on you for awhile.

Windows all the way down,
gas pedal held to the floor,
the rain-battered road promising
to curve sharply sometime soon.

Emily Dickinson's House

I went there once
but didn't go in.
Somehow it didn't seem right
to enter her bedroom.
She didn't want visitors then,
so why would she want them now?

So I stood outside
long after the house was closed
for the day, and I swear
that the curtain
of her bedroom window
was pulled back
for just a moment

the way I'm sure it was
when she held it
in her delicate hands.
I know it's not true—
but that doesn't matter—
I imagined she was still there

of and not of this rude place
called the world, white dress
that they show, that they say
she wore, and all the things
she possessed gathered together,
just as the words
I've come to know by heart
have come to rest
just long enough
(dare I say it?)
to change the world
at least for a little while,
at least for me,

each time I read them
or say them out loud
to myself as I imagine she did
when she stood by the window,
white dress lighting,
echoing, shattering the room.

Heritage

You were smiling the day you came home
wearing your new teeth and started talking
about apples: "No more applesauce!"
Later, you had given up wearing them:
"Never fit good anyhow."
And the apples weren't as good
as when you were a boy
climbing Doc Tucker's trees.

The saws you owned are mine now,
and I work wood like you and your father,
a line unbroken for eleven generations
until your son sold vacuum cleaners
and aluminum siding door to door
then settled down to used cars.
I build porches the way you taught me:
the bottom rail low enough
so a milk bottle won't roll off.
Grandfather, milk comes in cardboard containers
or plastic jugs now,
and milkmen are as rare as porches
with people sitting on them after supper
the way we used to.

Yesterday I built a small porch,
trading my labor for a cider press and made cider
thinking of you, how we'd go to the orchard
and basket home apples
then squeeze sweet cider out of them
in the press you built before my father was born.
You let me struggle against the wheel
you knew I could not turn then placed
your warm hands over mine and said,
"Must be stuck. Let's see
if we can get it going."

I remember your hands. I'd look at them
believing mine would never get that big
or do as many things. The last time
I saw them, touched them,
they were no longer warm.
They were strung with Rosary Beads.
Fingers woven through each other,
hands folded across your stomach.

There are things I do now
the way you used to. I use my hands
in ways you taught me
without using words.
Sometimes I feel something warm
close over them. Like today,
when I was turning the wheel,
pressing apples the way we used to,
your hands closing, gently, over mine.

Wellfleet: A Love Story

No matter what else you believe about me,
right now I'm just a man lying on the beach.
I'd prefer that you think of me,
at this moment, on the outer edge
of Great Island on a day
near the end of April where I look up
every once in awhile to see
where my wife is off in the distance
picking up some things that belong to the beach,
putting some of them down, and some of them
in her pockets to make them belong to her
and to show me later when we coincide,
not because we have an abiding interest
in the same destiny, but because we want to.

I'm waiting for her to turn and wave to me,
a traveler who turns just before entering
a plane about to depart from a small airport
where passengers have to walk across the tarmac
and climb some silly stairway bolted onto
a pick-up truck right-angling the plane.
I wave back to let her know she's safe
here with me on the look-out
because I'm big and tall and maybe still strong
enough and maybe even intimidating enough
to ward off any wayfarers who might choose
to make this lovely beach a weapon,
their intent to wreak havoc by throwing
sand dollars as far out to sea as they can
or some other observable dastardly mayhem
on such a beauteous, caressing,
mid-week Spring day, balmy on all sides.

But there's only two women
who passed by awhile ago,
and I'm pretty sure I could take them,
with my wife's unabiding, devoted,
enthusiastic participation, of course,
(if it has to come down to that)
talking as they head toward Jeremy Point
because it's available now.
You have to be on a first-name basis
with that well-oiled moon's schedule
to get there at certain times of the day
or else be willing to participate
in a very moist waist-deep time-out
before being allowed back on shore.
Now in the distance one of them
gestures broadly as she talks,
an orchestra conductor way off tempo
to the waves that also have something to do
with the moon, rocking back and forth
over each other all along this longitude and latitude
that used to be but no longer is my home.

Lying back down away from the tumult,
I rejoin my paused vocation of making sense
out of the few clouds purring overhead,
those taunting shape-shifters who won't stay still
long enough to freeze them forever
into a pony throwing its rider before becoming
a boat on its way to discover America—
conveniently paused right down here
beside and, probably, beneath me—
some of the sailors jumping overboard
after their threadbare sombreros feathering away
but mainly because they know the flat earth's ocean
will shortly waterfall them far far from home,
and they'd rather take their chances
with a deepening belief that tides
will wash them up—baby ducks bobbing

to a fragrant shore—where flower-laden natives
will welcome and will not eat them.

I'll probably exit this occupation in a little while,
get up and join or not join my wife,
maybe at least go somewhere near her
so the two women, now on their way back,
won't see me as someone who might interrupt
their lives in some menacing or recreational way.
And I'm assuming it's still the same one
who is still talking with her hands
maybe interpreting for the woman walking beside her,
inventing a language of the hands
because she's used up all the words
she's ever had an acquaintance with
but still has plenty to say.

This excursion, so redactive, comes
to its logical conclusion: the sun sets,
our *Oohs* and *Ahhs* follow us back
to the aptly named Seaside Motel,
photographs yet to be developed
will be placed in an album my wife
will hand-letter some evening in winter
slowed down almost to a stop with snow,
and that we can open anytime we want to,
this wife of mine and me,
in a future that includes us,
and the shells and stones and beach glass
and small bits of wood that once had
another life far from here
and the feathers and bones she emptied
from her pockets that day,
a magician closing up shop for the evening,
tethered to memories threading us
from there to here
in such an admirable way,
together and forever walking

hand in hand, hand in hand
on our way home to our home
inland from the sea.

—for N.K.H.

Patience

This morning
I placed four small bowls
on a table
near the window
to catch the rain
leaking from the ceiling.

This evening
I found four small moons
deep in the bowls
and decided to wait
until morning
until the moons recede
to empty them.

Maybe

What can I tell you that you don't already know?

I mean, I know you know the sound of a touch
    upon a woman's skin.

Low on her back you hear the voice of her body
    saying, "More," saying,

"You always know." I know you know this
    because I imagine at one time

it was my hand, it was your body that called,
    "Again," and you know

that touch remembered itself the exact same way
    but added something new, something

that had not been done before so that voice
    had to learn new words to say

because each touch, each voice, each word,
    each hand was new

or is becoming new, just as each moment is new
    but will soon drift off

into memory, one or ones that will bring a smile
    when you are alone, remembering

that voice, that word, that hand, that touch.
    I know you know this

because someone who knows you knows who was there—
    maybe me, maybe you.

Maybe us. Maybe us. Maybe us.

Blue Chalk

The young girl sits all morning
looking at the blue,
dreaming of owning the blue.
When she's all alone
in the room she takes it.
She can barely close her fingers
around it as she walks
back to her desk.
She wraps it carefully
in a brown paper towel
and places it in the book
open on her desk.
She cannot close
the cover because the chalk
is so big, but thinks
it's still hidden even though
the book, held open,
is in plain sight right there
on her desk.
When she comes back
from recess, the book is closed,
the chalk back in the tray
beneath the blackboard.
She sits waiting for the teacher
to say something to her—
in front of everyone—
about what happened.
But the teacher doesn't say
a word about the chalk,
how she found it in the book,
how she took it back.
And the day goes on,
goes so slowly on.
After school
the young girl walks home

by herself on the sidewalk
she thought would have looked
so nice colored blue
like the sky, like water,
like birds she sees
moving through the air
that surrounds her,
that deepens around her,
as she moves through a world
that's somehow not as beautiful
as she knows it could be.

—for N.K.H.

Similes for the Sun

I'm certain that once in awhile—
maybe out of habit,
perhaps out of spite—
like someone intoxicated,
the sun staggers around
in the leafless branches,
the bark-tightened branches,
before shredding itself to bits
way off in the distance,
a distance so far away
that it can't be named properly,
though someone tried once
and called it the horizon—
you know, that place
that can never be reached
because when you get to
where you believed it was
it's still always something
that can only be pointed to.

Maybe it only seems to happen
this way on occasion,
the sough of that light
that comes mishandling
its own expectations,
getting tremulous, nervous
as a schoolgirl who has
not done her homework
for the first time, not knowing,
yet, that it will become a habit,
something that can't be broken.

It's just like that,
if you want to know.
Just like itself—lush,
reverberant, sightless—
like a blind man with a cane
gently tapping everything
ahead of himself,
going around that
which he cannot step over,
before continuing on
then vanishing without a trace,
not even leaving an echo
to prove he was here,
leaving us nothing
except a rumor, a feeble promise
that he will return and run
his lucid hands over us
and all the places
we call home.

Places Near and Far

I would prefer that it be Spain
if not Portugal now,
a shiver of sun, say,
to keep me warm.
The houses white
or embarrassingly pastel—
you know what I mean.

I would eat oranges
and, except for breakfast,
drink wine at every meal.

I would walk into town
in the morning
shortly after eating
just for the exercise
and once a week
to see if there's any mail.

Or perhaps swim in the sea,
the beach deserted,
the men who fish
miles out by now.

In the afternoon
I'd read poetry,
if I were so inclined,
the book dropping to my chest
as I sleep beneath
the olive trees
in which birds
I'm trying to learn the names of
sit avoiding the sun
as we all do
this time of day.

But it's only Tucson
and there is no sea,
the sun is relentless
and birds I still don't know
the names of
sit in the trees
beneath which I sit
reading poetry,
as I'm inclined to do
this time of day,
before falling asleep
in the shade.

Pantoum Beginning with a Line by Louise Bogan

Women have no wilderness in them.
It seems so final, but sometimes we cannot say,
"Listen, sometimes the trees speak to them"
because it would not be true for all women.

It seems so final, but sometimes we cannot say
anything. As much as we want to believe it
or because it would not be true for all women,
we have to be careful to talk of women or words

or anything. As much as we want to believe it
or pretend that women in the woods are afraid,
we have to be careful to talk of women or words
or the sky as it descends slowly into the trees.

Pretend that women in the woods are afraid.
Imagine that they are alone. There's no one near them
but the sky as it descends slowly into the trees.
That changes everything, even the women, eyes closed,

who imagine they are alone. There's no one near them
but they want to tell how it is the sky
that changes everything, even the women, eyes closed,
who lean into the darkness, finally, as if they could do nothing else.

They want to tell how it is the sky
that takes them in, encourages them
to lean into the darkness. Finally, as if they could do nothing else,
they lie down. After all, it is the wilderness

that takes them in, encourages them
to deny what they can no longer accept.
They lie down. After all, it is the wilderness.
It enters them gently. They begin to sleep.

They deny what they can no longer accept:
women have no wilderness in them.
It enters them gently. They begin to sleep.
They listen. Sometimes the trees speak to them.

Home

After you've chosen the house,
go in. Go in and close the door.
Now sit on the couch.
Fold your hands in your lap.

If the door cannot be opened,
go in through the window.
Go in and close the window.
Now sit in the chair
across from the couch.
Cross your legs,
perhaps right over left.

Now that you are comfortable,
turn on the lamp, the one
nearest to where you are
sitting on the couch or chair,
hands folded, legs crossed.

Someone will awaken
when the lamp comes on,
when the light rushes
from the room.
And when they call,
"Who's there?"
say nothing. Just sit still
on the couch or chair,
hands back in your lap,
and wait until they call again,
but still say nothing.

When you hear them coming
down the stairs, or down
the hall, turn off the lamp.
Open the window or door
and leave just as they enter
the room, just letting them
see your coat as it brushes
the sill.

And let them
hear you sobbing
as you cross the perfect lawn
so they will understand
that your need is great,
and that they can do nothing,
they can do nothing to help.

II.
The Tooker Paintings, First Series

Doors

Three doors open onto the hall.
The one on the left isn't open very far,
but the most light comes from that room.
So much light that the edge of the door
washes out. The doorknob's shadow
reaches diagonally across the lower panels
and looks like an oar, a paddle held
in mid-stroke, someone rowing through
this brief pool of light.
From the door on the right,
a woman is emerging.
Except for the robe draped over
her right shoulder, she is naked.
Her hair swept back, she puts
her right foot into the hall and looks
toward the lighted room. She looks
past the middle door, the one
that is wide open, the one
that leads to the darkest room.
But that's the room that holds
the most promise because
someone is sitting on the edge
of the bed, the bed that can't be seen,
sitting, so casual, the sheet draped
across the figure's lap. From here
only the left lower leg can be seen,
only the left forearm resting on the knee,
only the edge of the rug,
only the blackness that surrounds
everything else.
The woman is in motion,
moving from one room
to the next, moving from
what has just happened
to what is about to happen.

The seated figure is her lover,
I have decided, and they
are about to make love.
It is the middle of the afternoon,
that's why the light is so bright.
She is on her way to close the door
of the light-stunned room,
just as she's about to close the door
of the room she's leaving now,
before entering the middle room,
before she moves, dropping the robe
she holds over her shoulder,
to her lover. I can't decide
whether it's a man or woman
who sits so patiently. You see,
the middle room is so poorly lit
and the person who waits,
sits in that dim light,
sits so far back in the room
that I can't tell you who it is.
In fact, it's not important to know.
It is not important to anyone
but the woman as she moves,
as she moves toward the one
who desires her, who waits
for her, as she moves
from room to room,
making the darkness,
at least for now,
at least for them,
a place that begins
in whisper
and ends in touch.

Lovers

This embrace, this sudden hold,
begins where the sky begins

to come down, coming down
in its delicate, its deliberate blue,

where the lean and supple grasses,
yellow and tan, bend around them,

bend beneath them, beneath the deeper blue
of the blanket beneath them.

It begins when she lies down
and he lies on her, on her red dress,

his arms around her, her arms around him,
his face in her hair. He closes his eyes

and could almost weep because he is so happy,
because it has been so long since they held

each other like this, been so very long
since he kissed her hair that is the color,

the very same color, of the grasses bending
around them, so very long since he told her

how the sky begins to surround them,
how the blue around them closes in,

been so long since he told her, told her,
how the blue, how the blue begins.

Red Carpet

No one could doubt that the three young women
sitting on the edge of the carpet are sisters.
The shape of their faces, the color and length
of their hair, even their sleeveless dresses—
although of different shades—are the same.
The only difference between them
that you can see is the direction
in which they face as they sit
cross-legged on the floor, their bare feet
showing darkened soles.
They decided to come to this party
simply because it is summer,
and they agreed, just before entering,
that they would sit together
and would not speak,
not even to each other.

They do not like parties
but decided, recently, that they would
at least appear sociable and now
is as good a time as any to begin.
So they entered the room and sat down
just where the geometric patterns
bordering the rug move off at right angles.
Their feet touch the woven stars
spaced evenly across the carpet.
Smoke from their cigarettes
rises into the air. You cannot see
anyone else in the room but you know
the women are watching everything
that goes on and are celebrating
the distance between themselves
and their surroundings.

Though their faces are expressionless,
they have decided they want
all those who look at them to believe
they are artists. They think it makes them
appear exotic, and it is easier than pretending
they are from France or Spain because
they will not have to speak with accents
of how the light strikes them as it bursts
off the carpet like a flare behind a stalled car.
They want the other guests to think of
the word *brooding* so they sit as if
it was true. After all, it costs them nothing,
and, besides, it perpetuates a myth
and will give the others something to talk about
on their way home. But no one knows
that the women have decided—
even though they haven't spoken of it yet—
that they are not going to leave.

You think, for a moment,
that the sister who sits just behind
the other two has some doubts.
She holds her right hand
to her mouth. Of the three,
she is the one most likely to speak,
but she holds her tongue
because she knows by heart
those stories about the depth of blood
that creates a family and understands
colors, that's why she likes the carpet—
it's the color of blood.
Even though she believes she has been
placed here against her will, she will
do what her sisters want. She will
live by the decision to sit on the carpet
forever because she believes as they do
that artists have an obligation
to become the art they practice

even if it means they will eventually fade
just as the carpet around them one day will.

But they know this as well as you do—
when the incontestable sun sets
and changes the sky as it comes
right through the windows—
that the carpet will return
to that precious color that made them
sit down, that holds them perfectly still,
the smoke rising, always rising from
the cigarettes they hold in their slender hands,
artist's hands they would have you believe,
because they know you are capable of believing
whatever anyone tells you about them,
about their well-planned lives,
and how they decided—
no matter how dreadful the consequences,
no matter how much they will suffer,
as they know they will, as they know
all artists must—to live and die
for this terrible but beautiful thing
called the artist's life.

Gypsy

For her it's a day like any other.
She'll spend most of it
behind the curtain
that's suspended from a wire,
that breaks the room in two,
and is open just wide enough
to let someone enter. She sits
on one bentwood chair, her legs,
crossed at the ankles, on another.
You do not need her to tell you
where to sit. She will take her legs
off the chair when you arrive.

But before you get here
she spends her time staring
at nothing. She folds her arms
under her breasts and thinks
about another country
where olive trees ripen
not far from the sea,
where goats meander in a sound
of bells and hooves on stone,
where she had more important things
to do than sit and wait
to read someone's hands.

She thinks of the man
who came for her,
whose every word she believed,
who promised her a different life
if she would leave home
and follow him. Yes,
she's thinking of how different
this life has been. He stands,
arms raised, on the other side

of the curtain, just a shadow,
something disfigured
on the translucent screen.
From here it looks as though
he's reaching to touch her breasts
or to rest a hand on her shoulder.
It's difficult to know which
she would prefer he do.
In either case, she'd recognize
his touch and the promise
his hands once made.

But when you come here
you won't know any of this.
You have come here because
you have heard about this room,
about the small rugs that undulate
on the wall, of how the curtain breathes,
of how she will touch your hands
when she traces your life
as far ahead as she can see.

When you leave you will remember
this touch—her index finger
lightly following the lines
mapping your life—long after
she's told you that the one
you will meet will make promises,
will change your life,
will make you dream
of foreign lands, perhaps
one where olive trees ripen
so very close to the sea.

Builders

Although she can see how far along they are,
the woman has come to ask them
how much longer they will be working.
Barefoot, she stands in the doorway
holding one hand in front of her
as if she were holding a drinking glass,
but there's nothing in her hand.

Her husband stands near her, half-hidden
by one of the posts supporting the beam
that runs the width of the house.
I shouldn't call it a house, exactly.
A structure, perhaps, that's more like it,
because the building is very narrow
and the room is barely large enough
to contain the three men who stand inside
looking at her gesturing in the space
they built for a door.

There is only the bare frame of the building
so we have to imagine all the rest—
the walls, the roof, the windows,
and so on—all the things that define
where they are standing.
She stands on a small platform
that's only about six inches high,
but it is clearly meant to be the floor
of the building, although the boards
extend hardly a foot beyond
where she is standing.

The man she has come to see stands
with his right foot on the platform.
The other men stand on each side of him.
He holds a board waist-high as if it were a rifle

and he were a hunter crossing a field,
stepping over the furrows, trying to avoid
the cut stalks of corn that might crack
beneath his feet, warning off the prey
of one form or another he is seeking.

As the man and the woman look at each other,
her husband looks at the space between them.
He knows he is being left out, but she knows
he will not say anything to either of them
even if he knows what is happening
and what has happened between them.
This is one of those moments when
they all know that no one needs to speak,
that's why silence is the language they all share,
even the men who stand almost as sentinels
to this gathering, not sure what role
they are being asked to play, to witness,
and they wonder what they will say
to themselves, and maybe to each other
afterwards, after what is happening now
comes to whatever end it has to come to
when one or all of them turn away.

The man holding the board knows
what the woman wants. He knows
what to say to her, and when, and how
to say it. And when she looks at him
she wonders about the difference
between this man and the man she married.
She wonders how some men can provide
what other men never learn. But she doesn't know
what her husband knows or that he has learned
that by saying nothing, at times such as these,
he's giving her what he believes she needs.
One day will she thank him for it,
he wonders. Will she thank him,
and what will he say then? That is

the only thing he does know now—
that he might not know what to say.
If she is still there, will he know?

III.
In Japan

In Japan

the essential character
of an autumn moon

turns out to be a woman
who does not sleep

while waiting in vain
for a lover

as the night waits
and the wind darkens

to a degree
we cannot imagine

First Snow

Tonight, while the season's first snow begins,
I look through a book of paintings

done by Hiroshige in 19th century Japan.
In this painting the houses are covered with snow

and peasants walk bent over
under woven hats while snow begins

to drift around them and fattens
the thatched roofs. The yellow glow

of oil lamps in the village windows
dimly show the way home.

But no one seems to be going home.
Instead, they are walking, letting themselves

be shrouded in snow. Their only purpose now
is to watch it come down and gather

upon itself and on each other.
In the houses children dress

in thickly padded clothes.
They'll be going out soon

because they've said to each other
since it first started to fall, "Come,

let's go snow viewing until we're buried,"
knowing that Bashō said it first,

but they like to think
they're the first ones to say it

because it reminds them of when
they were discovered by the snow.

Snow

> *It is surely my child*
> *who is shouting in the snow.*
> —Arō

who is shouting in the snow
is it my child

is it
my snow child shouting

shouting in the snow
who is my child

my shouting child
in the snow

it is the snow shouting
it is my child

surely it is the snow
who is

shouting
shouting

it is
the snow

the shouting
snow

Viewing the Moon

Sometimes it's so simple:
the blue heals itself quickly
around the husk, the sloughed off scar
we call, not as desperately as some believe,
the moon—old friend, damp light,
sudden river spooling out another story
until it comes to the final curved trace
of itself, a slight rim of white
tipping while it rises and sets.

And beneath it I think of the pleasure
of the Japanese, at least years ago,
who would invite guests over
to look at the moon, walking out
on a small bridge, perhaps over a stream,
or just in their gardens,
tipping their heads in unison,
their faces washed by the thin light
that makes everything beautiful
and staggers lovers,
as it's supposed to do,
who stand arm in arm,
sometimes for hours,
viewing the moon.

Parting

I think it was winter when you asked me
if you should cut your hair
and I said no because your asking
made me think of the woman who wrote,

> *Everyone tells me*
> *my hair is too long.*
> *I leave it as you saw it last—*
> *disheveled by your hands.*

I don't remember her name,
only that she lived in Japan
a few centuries ago.

Watching you that night
as you combed your hair,
I thought of those lovers,
of how much his touch meant to her
and how much yours meant to me.
And I remember that I thought
of how you would look later,
when we would make love.
Like so many other times
I would move my hands
through your hair as you moved
above me and you would roll
your head to your chest
then tip it back, your hair spilling
through my fingers.

Just now I opened my hands
and thought, for a moment,
that I could feel your hair
moving as it did those nights,
but it was just something

my hands remembered.
Still, I'll take that memory
if it's all I can have
because it reminds me
of how you looked when I saw you
for what would be the last time,
your dark hair flowing
through my hands.

And I can say, because it's true,
that it seems as if it was centuries ago
that I sat for awhile,
after answering your question,
watching you comb your hair,
before moving to your side
to take the comb from your hand.

Postcards from Japan

1.
Warm enough so I can leave
the windows open all night
to hear what is probably the wind
sighing through the leaves.

2.
Because my wife is sleeping
I have no one to talk to right now
except the moon
who woke me with a gentle hand.

3.
They must have come in as eggs
clustered on the water plants
I bought for our small pond—
fifteen goldfish I catch
and bring in for the winter.
Too many to name.

4.
Usually I sing in the morning
after getting out of bed.
It bothers my wife,
but not as much as it did
my first wife—
she didn't like it at all.

5.
My grandfather's carpentry tools.
Once I didn't know
what to do with them.
Now I do. Now I know
why I have these hands.

6.
Even though I don't have to,
even though I am no longer
a Buddhist monk,
I still get up at 4 a.m.
to keep the quiet company
so it won't be lonely.

7.
When I hit my thumb
with a hammer while building
the meditation platform
in the zendo, roshi said,
"Even monkeys fall out of trees"
to help me climb back up
the branches.

8.
Isn't it always O.K.
to slow dance
all by yourself,
with or without music?

9.
The front of this postcard
isn't blank.
It's what the snow
looks like here
where I am.
Isn't it beautiful?

10.
Wish I was here
where here is.
Come find me.

Teachings of the Buddha

I.

Cat jumps on my lap
and my book,
Teachings of the Buddha,
500 pages long,
falls to the floor
and closes—Thump!
Picking it up,
I can't remember
my place. Oh well,
must be time
to start at the beginning—
again. The cat
doesn't mind.
Neither do I.

II.

Cat jumps on my lap
and my book
falls to the floor.
Picking it up,
I find my place
easily, just like
my cat does:
my lap her lap,
book or no book.

III.

Cat jumps—
book falls.
How lovely
the snow outside.
Did I forget
to mention
the snow
before now?

—for K.C.

Paper Swans

1, Sasebo Japan, 1968

She could make swans
and other birds
with her hands,
and she gave them to me,
a sailor in another time and place,
going back soon
to an unpopular Asian war.

Her friend, another bar girl,
said to me later,
"She never gives them
to anybody. Why
did she give them to you?"

"I told her that her hands
looked like swans swimming
across the moon."

"Oh," she said.
"Good. Very good.
Like a poem."

2. New York, 2007

My wife came home
from a class
holding a paper swan.
"Look what I learned to do
today," she said,
gently handing it to me
as if it were alive,
just out of its shell.

I took it from her hands,
ones so familiar, especially
when they touch mine,
and—just for a moment—
like those in a place and time
so very far away.

IV.
Close to Home

The Comet, 1986

I've stayed up night after night
trying to see it
through a friend's telescope,
but I'm lost
when it comes to stars.
"Let's start with the dippers
and go from there,"
he says over the phone
when I call to say
nothing I'm looking at
in the heavens is moving.

So, instead, I've started
watching birds and women
through the telescope.
This morning I saw
a male cardinal at the feeder
in a neighbor's back yard.
It's cold and there's enough snow
that cardinals should be south
of here, but this one
is persistent and stays
where there's food.
Looking like blood
moving across the snow,
he drops down to peck up
the scattered seeds.
Ragged squirrels stutter
around him but he
doesn't give an inch.

It's funny, but I remember
when I was growing up
in the fifties and sixties
everyone called the comet
Hailey's—as if
it were spelled with an *i*,
not two *l's*. Things change,
or maybe we didn't
pay as much attention then.
And I remember that
people used to say
when a comet appeared
disasters would follow.

And a sure sign of war
was that women's dresses
got shorter. If this telescope
is right, the skirts
my neighbor's wife wears
rise well above her knees now,
as I discovered by accident
when I was watching the birds
at the feeder and she came out
to bring them food,
her legs perfect constellations.

I'm not worried about
coming disasters, only about
the ones that are already here,
the persistent ones: famine
in Africa, wars in
the Middle East and Afghanistan,
and closer to home,
my marriage breaking up.
It's got nothing to do
with the neighbor's wife
although my wife thinks it has.

If we do break up, I imagine
that in the future I'll do
what most of us do—
that is, not blame myself.
Instead, I'll say that
it was probably the comet.
You remember, the stars
were moving but
I could never see them,
believing I was just a victim
of things that were
supposed to happen at night,
that were always elusive
but left a residue,
like the markings of a trail—
burned into the night—
by a comet that changed
its name, arcing, creaking,
stuttering across the sky.

Tango Lessons: Buenos Aires, 2007

I'm wondering if I can brave the indentations
the sky has in store for me tonight
because it's almost time for traveling
to be the foremost thought in my mind

but that hasn't happened yet,
so I'll wait for a moment to see
how ravishing whatever it is that I need
to be ravishing is ravishing.

And I need a little time after rappelling
down another hemisphere
because I've always believed motion
includes distance, its fabled relatives waiting,

baggage in hand or nearby, evaporating
in the heat that is suddenly also pulsing
nearby. One can only count on misconception
for so long yet always be ready

for the inevitable change to muttered vowels,
consonants, and all the other things
that damage language, sliding
from tongue to tongue, in such a fluid way

that often needs explaining,
but I don't have time to do so now.
Light years ago I didn't think this way,
but suddenly someone, O.K., a woman,

tangoed in, throbbing into the narrow space
that goes by the name of my heart,
her staggeringly luminescent legs
showing a mind of their own, exiting

and entering a floor-to-ceiling slit in her
brain-ravaging, ruby scented, rain-sheer,
lava-flowing dress, glass-black high heels
threatening to penetrate the stratosphere,

talking to me, not needing translation,
over accordions and violins,
and then her hands, obedient
to memories of time, place, and distance,

somehow echoing the dimmed lights
strung overhead, part the music
shrouding where I sit.
A lifetime could begin right now

the bubbling cauldron called my heart
singing in my chest tells me,
and maybe it should be mine.
Then rising to the promise

of her shimmering body
smoothly liquifying before me,
combining motion and distance,
diffusing light, and closing

the even nearer distance between us,
I start to believe it does not matter
which one of us leads,
which one of us follows.

A Momentary Stay

I sit up late reading Rilke,
translated by someone
I know slightly
but who wouldn't remember me,
I'm sure—it's been years—
and I'd like to believe
I was a different person then.

My wife is sleeping
because she has to go to work
in the morning
while I stay at home
and read and go for walks
in the afternoon
before going to school
to tell my students
to write about what they know,
about what is important to them,
knowing I'm only talking to myself.

Soon I'll go into the bedroom
and lie down beside her
and she will wake for a moment
and move closer
when I put my hand
on her hip
then go back to sleep
as I lie awake listening
to her breathe.

But right now
I'm thinking about angels,
how Rilke often spoke of them
as if they had something to do
with the lives we lead,

as if sometimes they placed
an imperceptible hand—
so delicately that we won't be
frightened but reassured—
on one of our shoulders
to help us understand,
without knowing how or why,
that we are guided on a path
we haven't made
but believe we have chosen.

And that touch
makes the world tolerable
and even something
to tell others about,
which is why Rilke
bothered so much
to write about angels
and how they deserve our praise
at moments such as these.

Mr. Moto Takes a Vacation

He begins by making a plan.
He imagines every step of the journey,
calculating how far he will be from home
when he arrives at his destination.
He chooses the place from a scene
on a poster showing white beaches,
palms lifting slowly, the water so blue
its color could only be called "fierce."
But the woman walking in the water
just where it retreats after dampening the sand
seems preoccupied, as if she were waiting
for someone. "Of course it will be me,"
Mr. Moto decides as he plans
what he will say to her when they meet
that night at the bar of the hotel,
she sitting alone holding a drink
in one hand, the other moving a strand of hair
back into place. Her name is Danielle,
and she cares nothing for the diamonds
she wears but likes the way they look
against her tan. The ceiling fans
revolve so slowly they seem about to stop.
But they never will because it is the tropics
where people have been known to die
when the air gets motionless,
when shades are pulled down against the sun,
and insects snap into screens.
"But this is not the time to think
of such things," Mr. Moto tells himself
as he looks at the poster again,
sweat stains bleeding through his shirt
and through his white linen dinner jacket,
and thinks of how she will appear
the next morning as she prepares for a day
in the sun. He will sit in the shade

near the pool feeling how cold the ice
makes his drink as he rolls the slender glass
between his palms. He will not be the only one
watching her as she comes out into the sun,
out from the shade, the nearly audible shade,
and steps to the edge of the pool,
its blue a version of the sky without clouds,
that deep, and steps into the water
where it rings around her feet and shines
from the oil he's rubbed on her skin.
This is when she'll turn to him and smile—
"Just the slightest trace of a smile,"
he'll say to someone, later, when asked—
before she turns and disappears for good
beneath the waters of the pool of the hotel
where Mr. Moto's vacation comes to an end.

Listening to Bill Evans

is easy to do in the rain,
which is what it's doing now.
The rain may be listening too
because I have the windows open,
and I can hear it over "Waltz for Debby,"
but just barely.
And it's late Sunday morning
and the neighbors are restless,
squabbling as all good neighbors
can and should be doing because
isn't that part of the social contract
between neighbors who share
a common wall? One side
is always going at it and the other side
bangs on the wall and threatens—
yet again—to really call the cops
this time. We all have our roles
to play, but they do theirs
better than I do mine.
Meanwhile, Evans
is oblivious, and isn't that the way
it's also supposed to be?
I saw him play live once
and can picture him now,
his head nodding to the keys
then lolling back, eyes closed.
And because I know
by heart all the words of the neighbor's
"Yes you did! No I didn't!" song,
which is as far away from Evans
waltzing with Debby as you can get,
I close my eyes too right now,
because when the music is here
it also takes me somewhere else
and makes some wrongs right.

Not all of them, but just enough.
And if there was ever a time
to shut the windows
and turn up the volume,
that time is now.

Songs for the Tropics

In the place of the toucans
where the toucans grow
above the jaguars
where the toucans grow
bright shoulders against the sun
against the psalms
the jaguars sing
beneath the palms
the toucans do not grow old

In the place of the toucans
where the toucans
touch the sky
the toucan hunters
walk through rain
knowing the toucans
will not fly
when they call
"toucan"
to call the toucans down
in this place
where the jaguars wait

In the place of the toucans
where the toucan hunters reach
to touch the toucans
the sky recedes
as the jaguars touch
the toucan hunters
and the toucans
with their teeth

Heartland

When the sky dies in Elk Basin
a woman who just now is reaching
to take clothes from the line
stops moving.
Her left hand outstretched,
she looks off in the distance
across the bronze field
that moves beneath the damp hands
of the now rising moon.
She holds her breath and listens
for someone, not her husband
or children who sit silently
at the kitchen table,
to call her name.

She watches her hands
that are poised above the line
and remembers how in the night,
when she doesn't sleep,
they rise to lead a life of their own.
There is little she truly understands:
for instance, how the roses
print themselves against the sky,
or even simpler, how the sky lifts
the petals and lets them fall
through her fingers.

But tonight she knows
that when her husband,
without rising from his chair,
calls, she will not answer,
and when he comes to the door
and leans out, she will move off.
She can no longer watch
in amazement her scar-bright hands

tugging the wooden pins
from the clothes, those bright flags
of her children that tremble
with each touch on the line.

And as she begins to breathe
in this life she is inventing,
she hears her name being called.
She hears it beyond the crickets
calling females darkly to them.
She hears it as she moves
toward the black between the trees,
hands held out for the touch
she knows is there.

Out Here

Driving through the mountains
I fear avalanches
I fear wolves
if they'd come down
out of timber
and demand food

my hands a slender meal

at every rest stop
I bless my tires
count the lug nuts
and check the spare

my gas cap locked
against the sudden need
of deer

you can never be too certain
out here
where the snow comes early
deep and long

I see myself
caught in the blizzard
that calls my name
coaxes me out of the car
and freezes the engine
with the patience
of a glacier

I imagine I will be found
huddled beneath
the slowest flowing reach
of a spruce
as if it had given birth

curled to myself
speaking my last words
to my knees

what's left of me
ascending through snow
in spring perhaps
after animals being animals
have discovered me

bits of blue
that were my coat
no longer
keeping me warm

Shorelines

Once, when you said you had never seen the snow fall
into the sea, we drove three hours east to the Atlantic,
when a light snow was predicted, then crossed
the long wooden bridge at Powder Point,
the tires drumming the planks above Duxbury Bay,
then parked in the sand. Listening to the water

heave in time with that long tug from the moon,
we walked through the beach grass
until we could smell what we could hear
but could not see just beyond the rise of the low dunes
because the snow fell at a steepening angle,

curtaining everything around us, falling faster and harder
than we were led to believe. Then we were almost at the edge,
the end of the world. On another day all we could see
would be distance. Instead, there was just the softening
late-afternoon light, the nearing dark less than an hour away,
the snow, and you leaning into me, saying, "Listen.

I'm sure it's the sea. Are we that close?
It sounds like breathing. It's hard to see anything."
We had to turn back because there was too much snow,
relearning how dark coastal Massachusetts is at 4:30
in the afternoon in January as we drove over

to Plymouth to find a motel. This afternoon
I come here again, but now I'm by myself,
and this time the snow is falling slowly into the water—
gray, green, thick, ragged as always.
Today I see things I could not see that day
as we stood listening to the sound of what does not change,

not seeing that which does, or would, one day
in a future neither of us could predict, or,
as it turned out, forestall. Maybe the next time
I hear from you I'll remember to tell you
about this slowing winter day when I saw

the sea rise and heave its long shoulders
into the snow. And that, yes, it does breathe,
only you have to learn how to listen closely.
It's not difficult—because you learn how easy
things are when you have no other choice—like falling
in and out of love, it happens one breath at a time.

Close to Home

I'm a complete failure as a tourist,
and I'm terrified by language.
This one I speak fluently
frightens me most of all.
So much so
that places close to home
are no longer recognizable
or are rendered unfamiliar
by what can be said
about the throb of sky
interfering with the distances
that are supposed to exist—
where the trees creating a horizon
burst into flame
as the sun going down hits them,
where the current trend of rain
is so tiresome that even my dog
is irritable, unaccountably lonesome
because he believes he's missed
certain rites of passage
I told him about after reading
the latest *National Geographic.*

And when I consider
that the people in the country
from which I have a passport
speak a foreign language,
then I can't be blamed
for the delirium I feel
when I find myself
anywhere near an outpost,
airport, or port of call.
In short, it's a ruthless life
when the principle of individuality
is given such importance

that people take you
at your word, not knowing
that when we leave home,
if it weren't for phrase books,
our shameless trust in language,
we'd have to return
to that famous reliance
on gesture and touch
to make ourselves understood.

A Love Affair

"You write about hands a lot,"
she said,

not knowing
that as she was reading

I was
looking at hers—

so slender

so delicately
holding these pages.

—for N.K.H.

About the Author

Carpenter, cabinetmaker, house wright, mariner, luthier, teacher. M.F.A. University of Arizona. Ph.D. University at Albany, Robert Harlow taught literature for many years at the U. of Arizona and the U. at Albany. He is married to the ceramic artist, Nancy K. Henry. They reside in rural upstate NY on many wooded acres. He is the author of the collections, *Recitations Before the Dance Begins* and *Recollected Poems.*